AVA LEARNS TO BE COURAGEOUS

Ava Learns To Be Courageous

CHAPTERS

1 COLORFUL MOMENTS

2 SUMMER SURPRISES

3 MYSTERIOUS JOURNEY

4 FEARFUL MOMENTS

5 COURAGEOUS CHOICE

6 FEARFUL TO FEARLESS

7 DELIGHTFUL ENCOUNTER

8 HOOVES OF HAPPINESS

Dedication

I give glory and honor to Abba for enlightening me to rediscover myself. Without his guidance and constant source of strength this would not be possible.

Alicia, you have always motivated me to persevere, your encouragement has been my anchor.

To everyone, who has been my cheerleaders and inspiration throughout this journey, this book is for you.

To the young readers, whose love of reading keep these stories and books alive, may this book be a beacon of hope and inspiration on your own journey of discovery

AVA LEARNS TO BE COURAGEOUS

A Tale of Suspense!

Join Ava on her courageous journey as she learns to face her fears and discovers the beauty of friendship in the most unexpected places.

This book
belongs to:

Summary

In a town where every day holds a new adventure, meet Ava, the bright girl with a secret fear. Join her as she dives into a summer filled with excitements, with Aunt Kat by her side and Koda, her loyal dog. But what happens when Ava's fear comes face to face with her? Will she find the courage to overcome it, or will she hide forever? As Ava heart races and her stomach churns with fear, a mysterious encounter unfolds that will change everything. Who is this stranger on horseback, and what will Ava do when they meet? Will she let her fear control her, or will she discover the bravery inside her?

Filled with suspense and unexpected twists, this tale will keep you captivating until the very end. Can Ava conquer her greatest fear and make new friends in the most unlikely place? And what magical moment awaits her in the barn, amidst the beautiful horses? Follow Ava on her journey of finding courage and friendship, and how she unlocked the hidden secrets within her heart to overcome fear.

1

Colorful Moments

Ava was a bright eight years old girl with a mass of shiny hair and clear brown eyes.

She lived in the small and colorful town of Margaret River with her parents and dog, Koda.

Ava loved studying, painting, reading,
swimming, and playing with Koda.

She was a brave little girl who could do many things,
but Ava had one great fear: she was scared of horses.

2

Summer Surprises

Summer holiday arrived, and Ava was so excited. She couldn't wait to have great fun. Her Aunt Kat was visiting for the summer, and Ava loved her greatly. But Ava didn't know she would be forced to face her fears!

It was a lovely Sunday afternoon, and the clouds were spreading above. The sun pierced down on the trees as the branches swayed in the wind. Trees clustered in the woods, and birds chirped as they sat on the boughs, some flapping their wings, others chatting with each other.

"So beautiful," Ava whispered, smiling as she walked from church and headed home. The church was close to the house, so it wasn't unusual for her to walk by herself. "So beautiful," Ava said again.

3

Mysterious Journey

Right then, a gorgeous birdie settled on u
small tree in front of Ava, and she paused.
"Hello, birdie!"

Ava waved excitedly, but the bird flew away.
Ava followed the bird until she soon came
upon a crossroad alone.

"You got carried away again, Ava," she said to herself and sighed. Ava started to turn but stopped suddenly. She looked down the crossroad and began to imagine the distance it travelled. Whoa! How far would I go to see the end? Ava was curious.

It was a rugged dirt road with weeds scattered all around and buds blooming here and there. Ava stood staring at the crossroad.

Suddenly, she heard a sound. A strange sound.
Gallop! Gallop! Gallop!

What is that? Ava wondered. The sound grew closer and closer until it became a trotting sound. Ava listened carefully, and when she turned, she gasped in fright. It was a policeman on horseback! And he was coming closer.

4

Fearful Moments

She couldn't be seen by the policeman on horseback. She was sure he would stop, and the horse would too. Ava didn't want that.

Ava shivered, her heart raced, and her stomach began to ache a little. She was so scared.
Then quickly, she jumped behind the slope and lay down to hide.

The bushes shook a little as Ava moved and settled between them.
The trotting sound approached, and when they got to the area
where Ava hid, there was a halt.

Ava breathed heavily, overwhelmed with fear. She peeked between the shrubs and saw that the policeman was looking down. He heard the rumbling below the slope.

5
Courageous
Choice

Ava suddenly remembered her mum's words,
"It's okay to be scared. It's a part of growing up.
But don't let your fears control you; you're stronger
than that."

What would happen if I came out of hiding? Ava wondered. The policeman looked around for a moment and made a turn. They were about to leave.

Ava's heart wouldn't stop racing as she finally made her decision. She came out of hiding.

6

Fearful To Fearless

"Hello!"
Ava said timidly.
She still shivered
a little from
fright.
The policeman
stopped.
"Oh, Hello there!"

"Are you alright?" the policeman asked, concerned.
"Yes, I am. I'm just scared of horses," Ava said.

"Oh, it's okay. We all have fears. And you're a brave little girl who faced your fear," the policeman praised.
"I am?" Ava was pleased with herself.

Ava shook her head. "Thank you, sir, but I can go by myself," she said.
"C'mon, Can I take you home?" the policeman asked.
She may have faced her fear, but she was far from overcoming it.

"Alright, make sure you be on your way," the policeman said and galloped away.
Ava couldn't believe she had just seen a horse so closely!

When she got home, she told her parents all about it,
and they were shocked and excited for Ava.
"I'm so proud of you, honey," her mum applauded,
clapping.

7
Delightful
Encounter

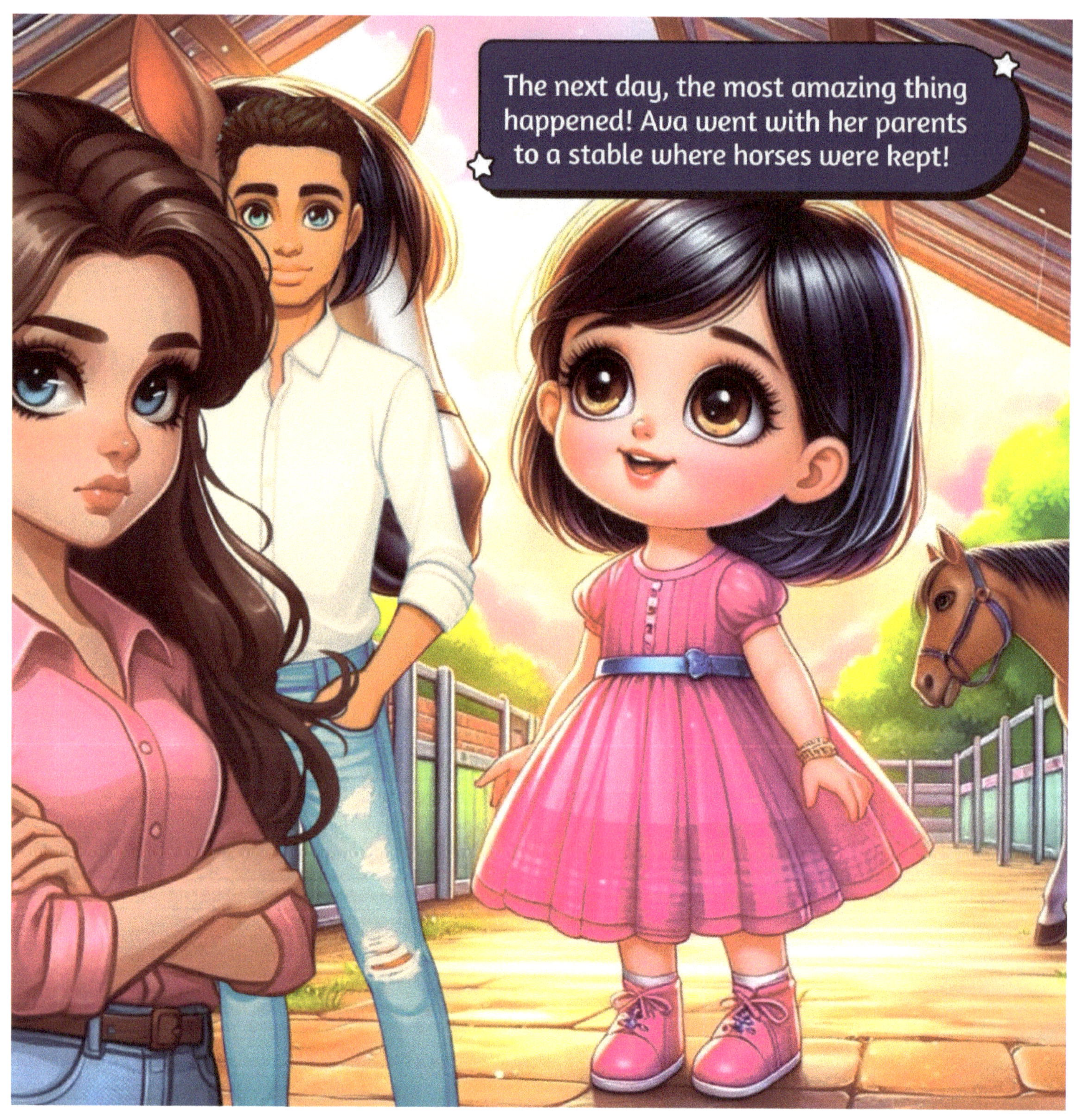
The next day, the most amazing thing happened! Ava went with her parents to a stable where horses were kept!

Though she was still scared of them, she was soon standing close to them, fascinated by their oval-shaped hooves, long slender legs, long thick necks, long tails, and their one-toed feet! She also found the mane, and the hairs on the neck of the horses, very interesting.

"They are so beautiful," Ava said delightedly.

"Yes, they are," her mum replied, smiling. "Do you want to touch them?"
"Yes, You can."
"I can?" Ava asked, a little scared.

Gently, Ava reached for the mane. "It's so soft," she said, smiling.
Ava's parents were excited to see their daughter smiling at the horses she had always been so scared of.

"So, do you think they'll be your new friends?" her mum asked gently.
"Yes!" Woo-hoo Ava exclaimed

8
Hooves Of Happiness

Ever since then, Ava became a girl who loved horses. Her fear was long forgotten. She learned all about them and could play with them all day!

Ava's parents decided to take her to the barn often so that Ava would be more acquainted with horses and to show her that horses are beautiful animals.

MORAL LESSON

Even the bravest hearts can have fears, but facing them can lead to wonderful adventures and new friendships. Don't let fear hold you back; be brave like Ava and discover the magic that awaits on the other side!

KIDS
Activities

Words Search

Summer

Fear

Horse

Bravery

Courage

Questionnaire For Kids

1. What is the name of Ava's dog?
2. Where does Ava live?
3. Who comes to visit Ava for the summer?
4. What is Ava's biggest fear?
5. What sound does Ava hear that makes her scared?
6. Who does Ava encounter while hiding?
7. What does Ava's mom say about fear?
8. Where do Ava's parents take her the next day?
9. What does Ava think about the horses after her visit to the stable?
10. How does Ava feel about horses at the end of the story?

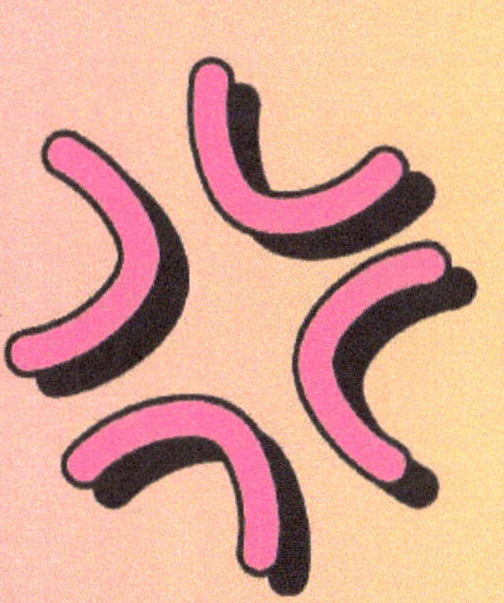

QUIZ
What is the name of Ava's dog?
A Max
B Koda
C Buddy
2×2

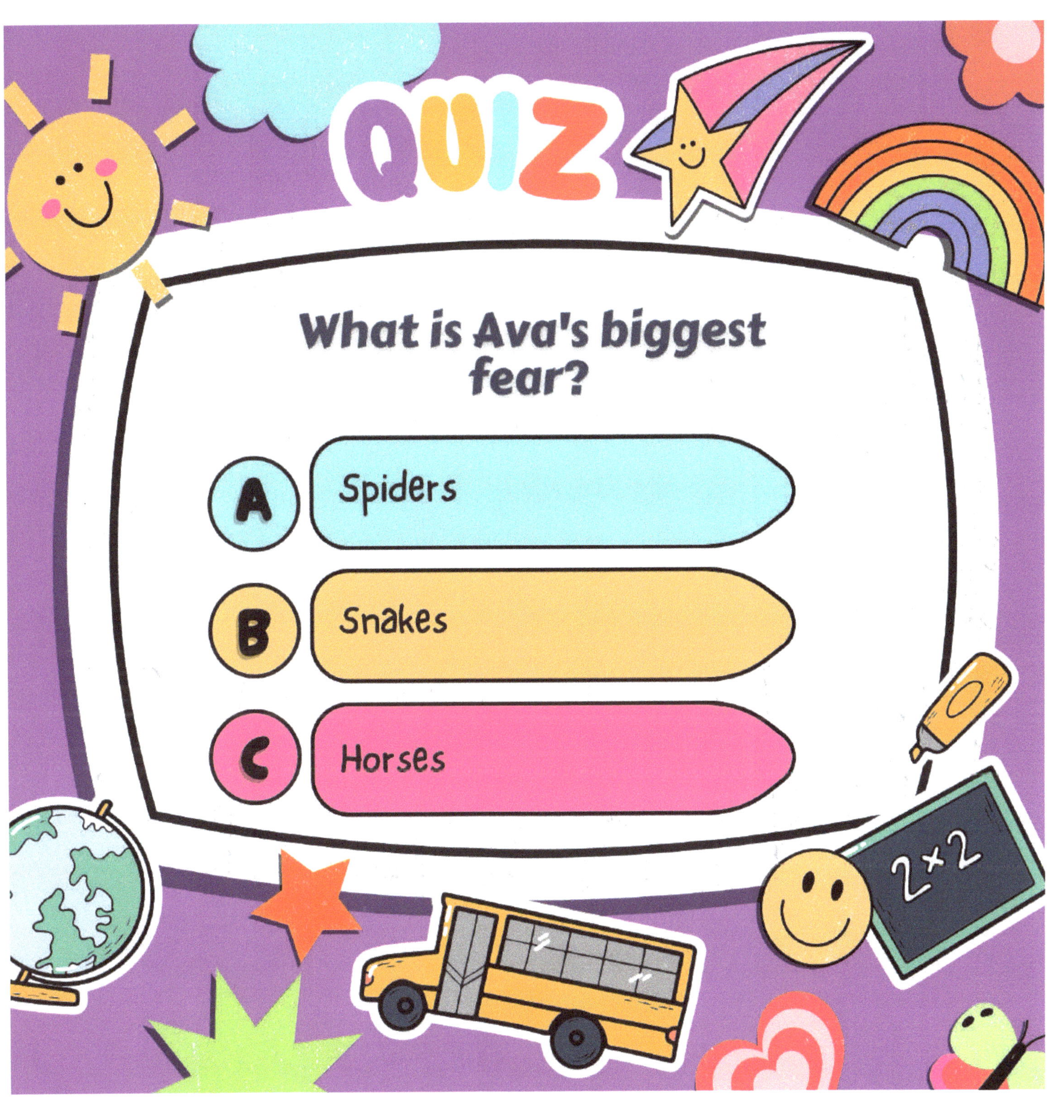
QUIZ
What is Ava's biggest fear?
A Spiders
B Snakes
C Horses
2×2

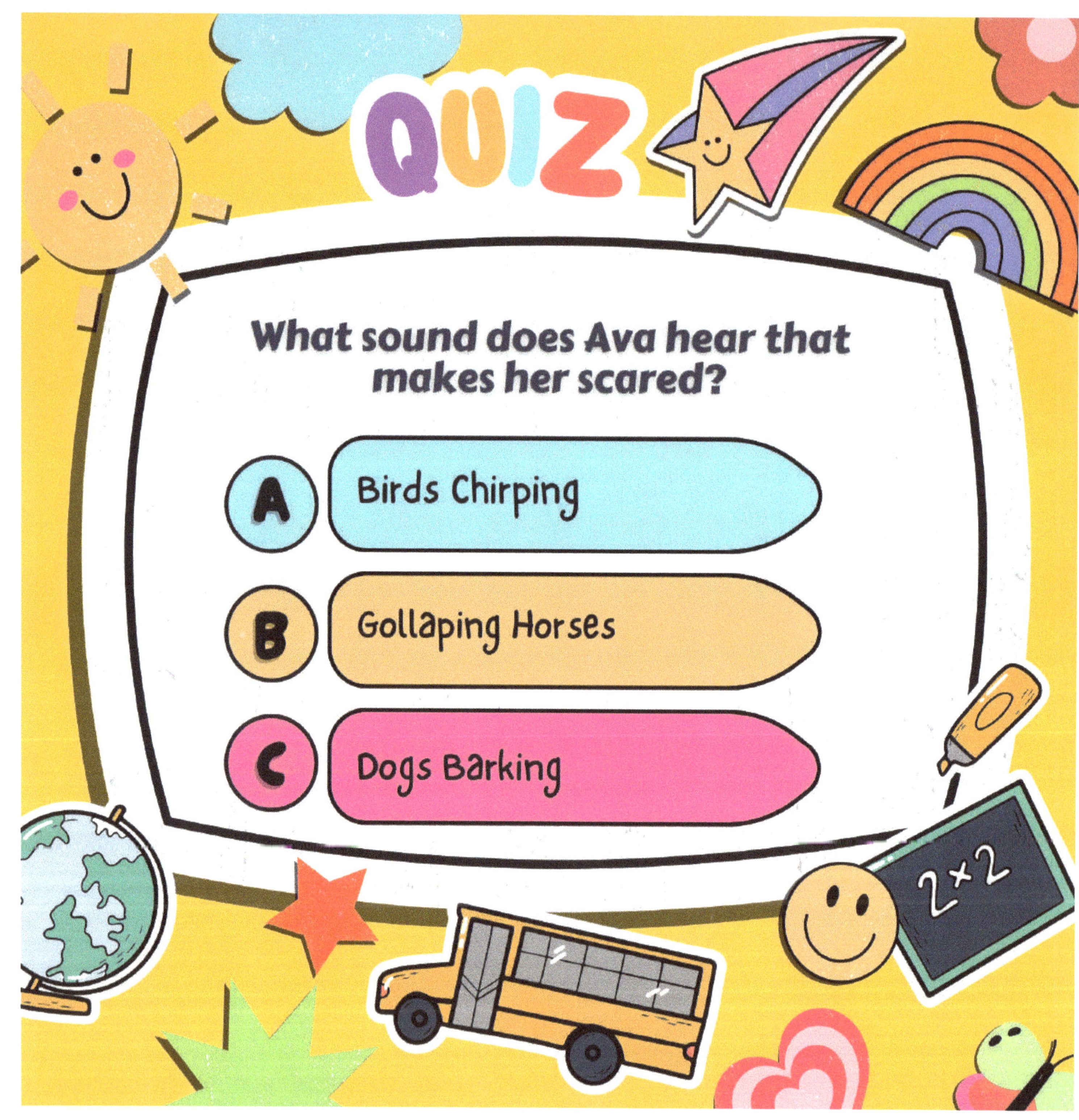

QUIZ
What sound does Ava hear that makes her scared?
A Birds Chirping
B Gollaping Horses
C Dogs Barking
2x2

Drawing Activity

Let your imagination run wild as you bring the colorful town of Margaret River to life on this drawing activity page! Capture the beauty of summer, the excitement of adventures, and the joy of new friendships with your artistic skills. Get ready to create your own masterpiece!

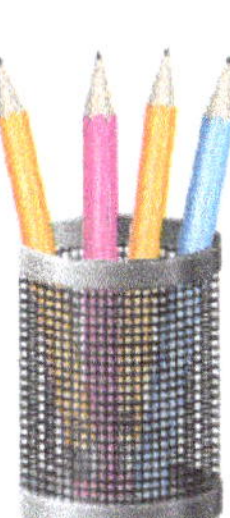

Writing Activity

Use your imagination to write about your own daring adventures and the friendships you've made along the way, just like Ava!

____

____

____

____

____

____

AUTHOR'S MESSAGE

Dear Kids!

As you turn the pages of this story, I hope you find inspiration in Ava's journey of bravery and discovery. Remember, even when faced with fear, you have the power to overcome obstacles and find new passions. Embrace each moment with courage and curiosity & let your own adventures unfold. May this tale remind you that true strength comes from facing your fears and finding beauty in unexpected places.

Best Regards
Enla Daniel

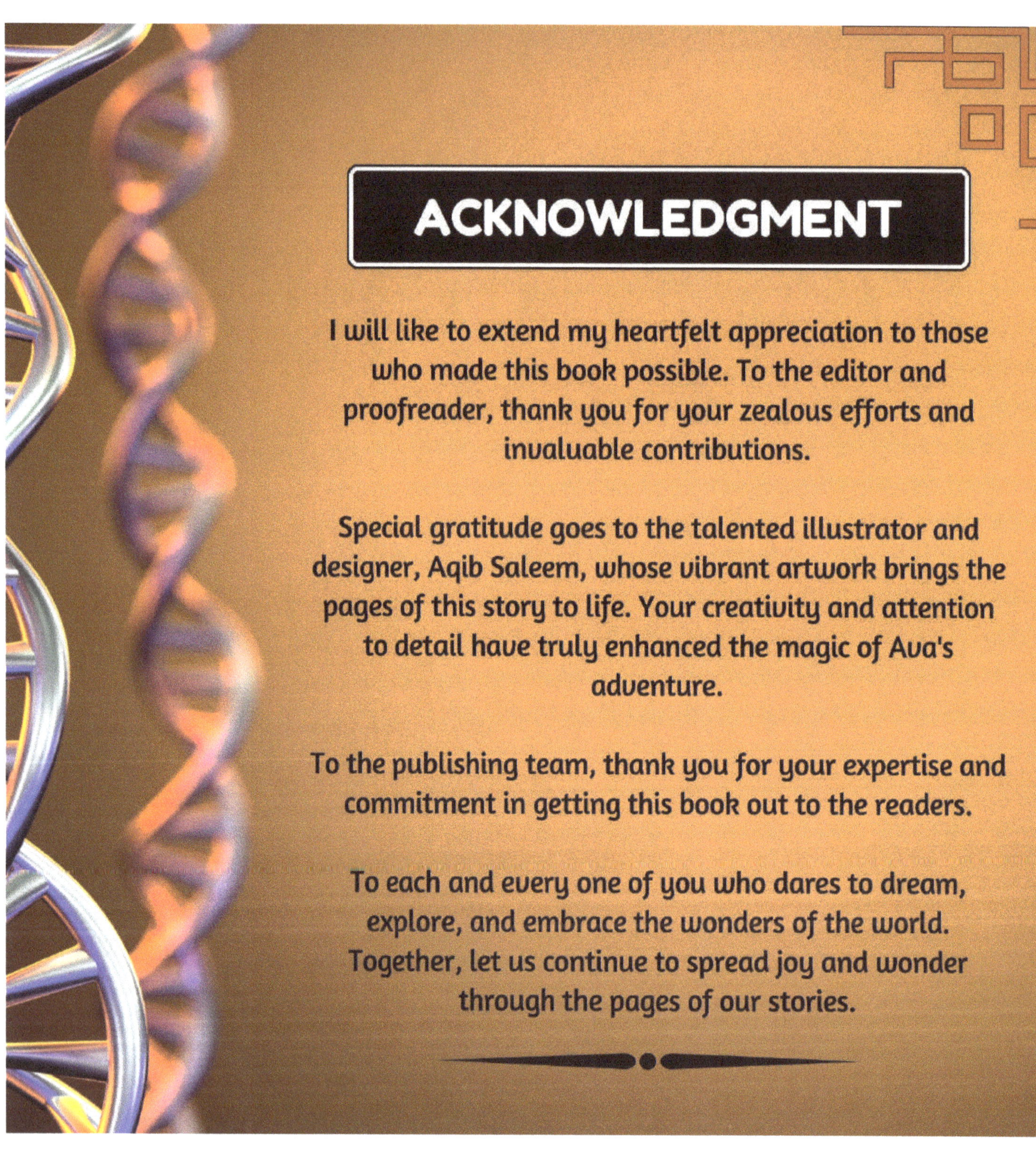

ACKNOWLEDGMENT

I will like to extend my heartfelt appreciation to those who made this book possible. To the editor and proofreader, thank you for your zealous efforts and invaluable contributions.

Special gratitude goes to the talented illustrator and designer, Aqib Saleem, whose vibrant artwork brings the pages of this story to life. Your creativity and attention to detail have truly enhanced the magic of Ava's adventure.

To the publishing team, thank you for your expertise and commitment in getting this book out to the readers.

To each and every one of you who dares to dream, explore, and embrace the wonders of the world. Together, let us continue to spread joy and wonder through the pages of our stories.

Testimonial
★ ★ ★ ★ ★
This delightful tale of bravery and friendship captivated my heart from beginning to end. The characters felt so real, and the message of overcoming fear resonated deeply with me. A must-read for children of all ages!
Emily L.

YOUR FEEDBACK

Share your feedback on this story book to help us improve.

Rate This Story Book

Dear Supporters

Thank you for reading our book.

Our key purpose is to provide interesting
& creative book to readers around the globe.

I would appreciate it if you could share your
opinion about this book. Additionally, if you
have the time, would you be willing to check
out my other books as well ! Thank you.